Merry Christmas

....

....

....

HO, HO, HO!

If you find this joke book in anyone else's hands, kindly remind them that Santa's Little Helper is the official owner of this jolly collection of Christmas hilarity.

Your mission is as clear as Rudolph's nose on a cold winter night: to spread more laughter than Santa's belly can handle.

Remember, it's not just about the presents under the tree but also Christmas cheer shared with glee.

WP Word Problem

R Riddle

J Joke

T Trivia

⚠️ Answers are located at the bottom of each page, cover it if you do not wish to see.

J What do grumpy sheep say on Christmas?

R I'm mean and green and stole Christmas scene. Who am I?

Baaa Humbug / The Grinch.

R
What does a Christmas tree have in common with Santa's beard?

T
What two phrases will you almost always find on Christmas gift tags?

Both need trimming. / To and From.

T
What Christmas movie has made the most money of all time?

R
In a wooden stance, he guards the night
With a jaw so strong, he's ready to bite.
Who is he?

J
Why don't sleds ever get tired?

Home Alone. A Nutcracker. Because they always go downhill!

> **Which reindeer can jump higher than a house?** — J

> **What do snowmen eat for lunch?** — J

> **In "The Twelve Days of Christmas" song, how many gifts were given in total?** — T

All of them, a house can't jump! / Icebergers / 364.

WP 6 kids made 6 snowmen.
If each kid made an equal number of snowmen,
how many snowmen did each kid make?

Find one hidden reindeer.

I am a ball that does not bounce. What am I?

R

What did the gingerbread man use for covers on his bed?

J

What do elves call pictures of themselves?

J

A snowball / A cookie sheet / Elfies.

J What do you call a cat on the beach on Christmas?

T What is the name of the Grinch's dog?

R I am not a sock, but I keep your toes warm. What am I?

Sandy claws. / Max. / A boot!

J: If you throw a white winter hat into the Red Sea, what does it become?

R: I wrap presents, but I am not an elf. What am I?

R: What normally comes once in a minute, twice a week, and once in a year?

Wet. / Wrapping paper. / The letter 'E.'

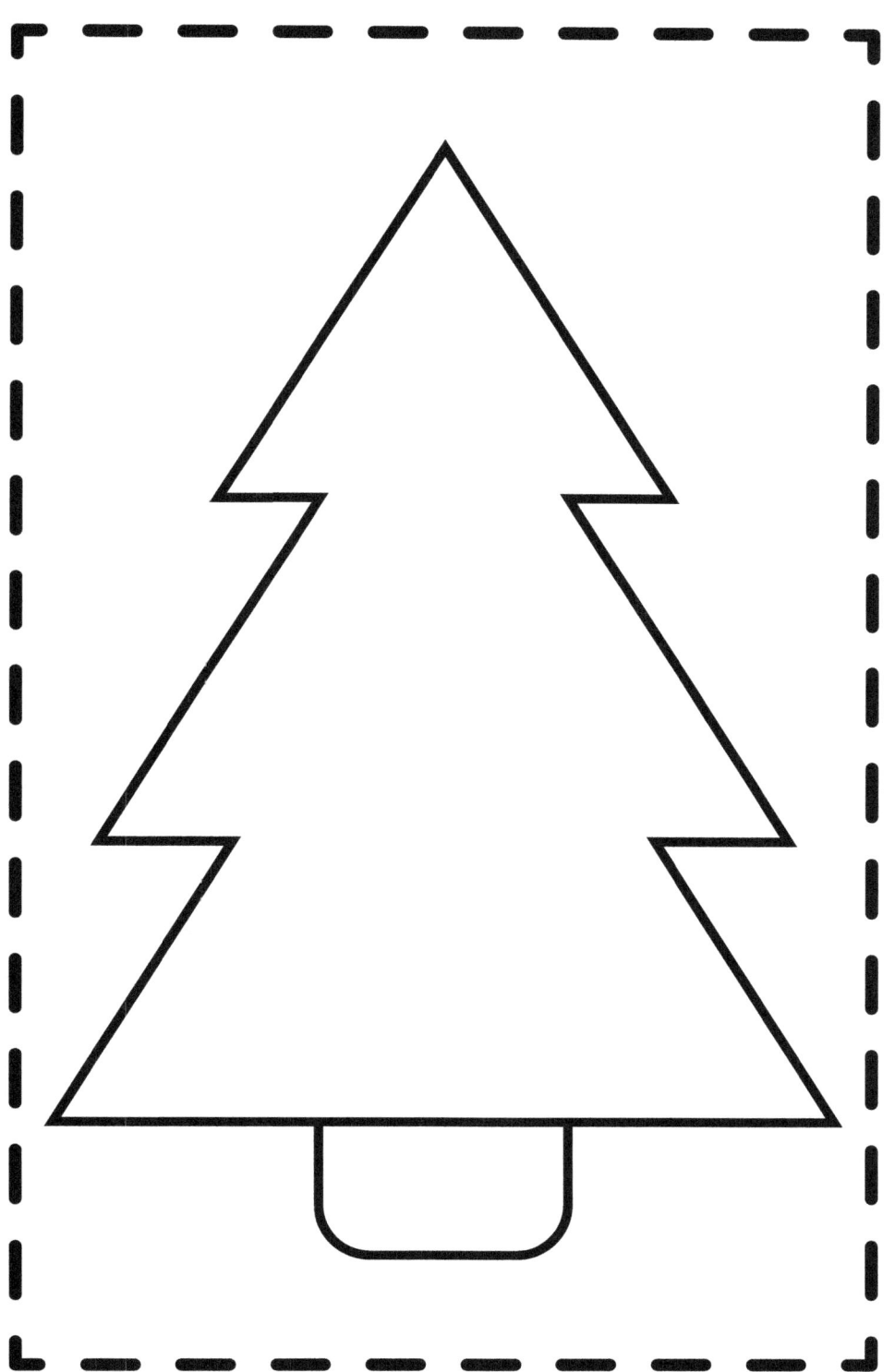

R Made of sweets and frosting so fine, a sugary home where candies align. What am I?

J What do you call Santa when he loses his pants?

A gingerbread house. / Saint Knickerless.

WP John has 20 candy canes. He gives half to his friend. How many candy canes does John have left?

J What says "Oh Oh Oh"?

J Where do elves go to vote?

10. / Santa walking backwrads / The North Poll.

R I once grew in the dirt, but now I wear a fancy skirt. In a stand you must insert. What am I?

J How do we know Santa is an expert at karate?

T Who is Santa's wife?

Christmas tree / He has a blackbelt / Mrs. Clause

Jingle Bells

J: What's the first thing that Santa's elves learn in school?

T: Which famous Christmas character goes around saying, "Bah humbug!"?

R: Hang me up high and stand below, a lover's kiss will surely bestow. What am I?

The Elf-abet. / Scrooge. / Mistletoe.

Emily baked 12 Christmas cookies. She ate 3 and gave away 2. How many does she have left?

She has seven left.

J: How does a snowman get around?

J: Which reindeer likes to clean?

T: How do you say "Merry Christmas" in Spanish?

He rides an icicle. / Comet. / Feliz Navidad.

J How can Santa's reindeer deliver presents during a rainstorm?

R I'm white and cold; and can be rolled to make a winter friend. What am I?

T Which classic Christmas song was originally written for Thanksgiving?

His reindeer are used to rain, dear! / Snow. / Jingle Bells

Decorate me!

J: What do you get if you cross a bell with a skunk?

WP: If Santa has 9 reindeer and they each eat 2 carrots, how many carrots do we need to leave out for all the reindeer?

T: How many times does Santa check his list?

Jingle smells. / 18. / 2 times.

T

In the song, "12 Days of Christmas," what gift is received of the 8th day?

J

Why did the snowman call his dog Frost?

Because Frost bites! / Eight maids a milking.

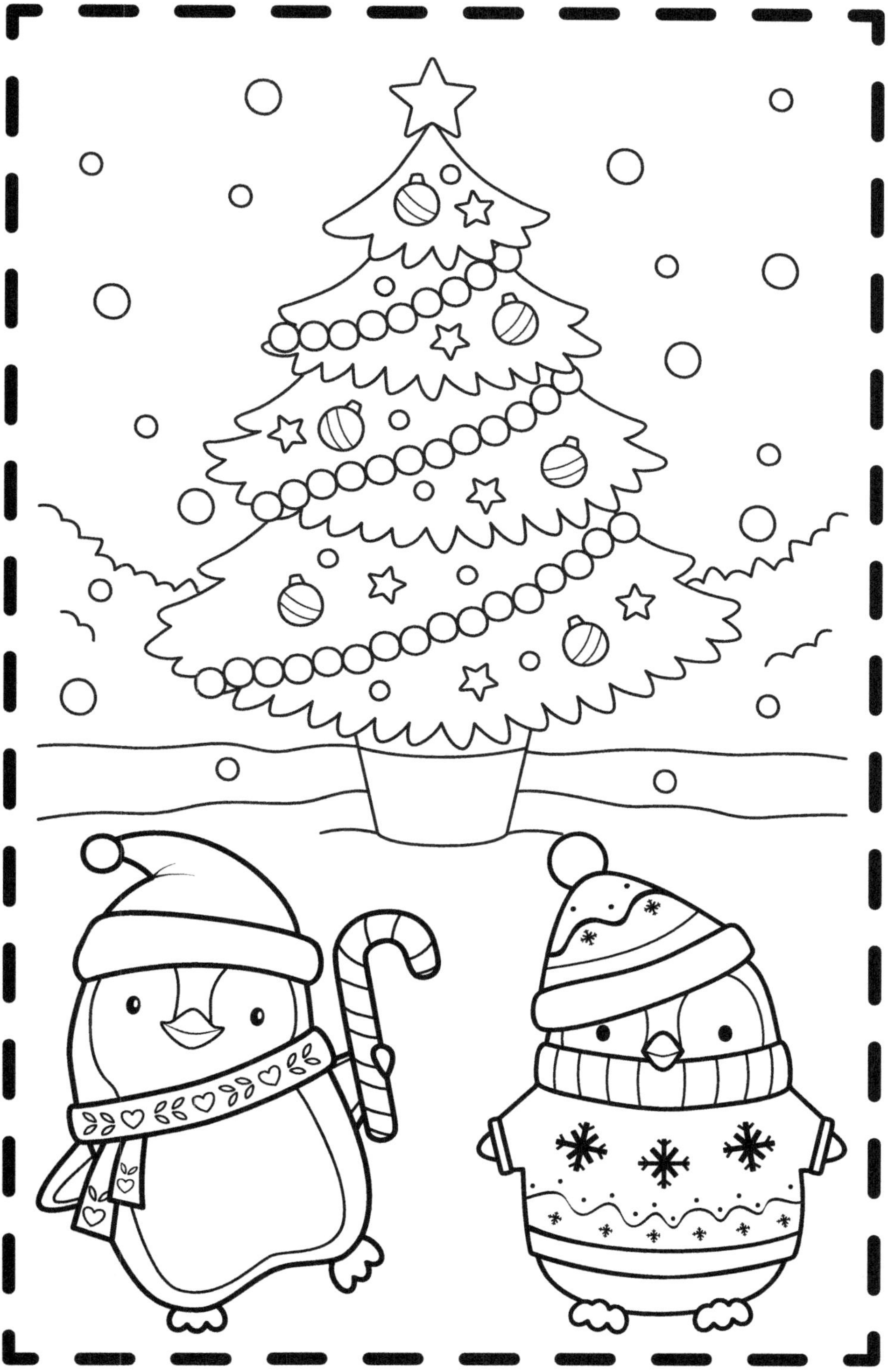

What do you call a snowman with a six-pack?

Why did the Christmas cookies visit the doctor?

An abdominal snowman! / They were feeling crummy.

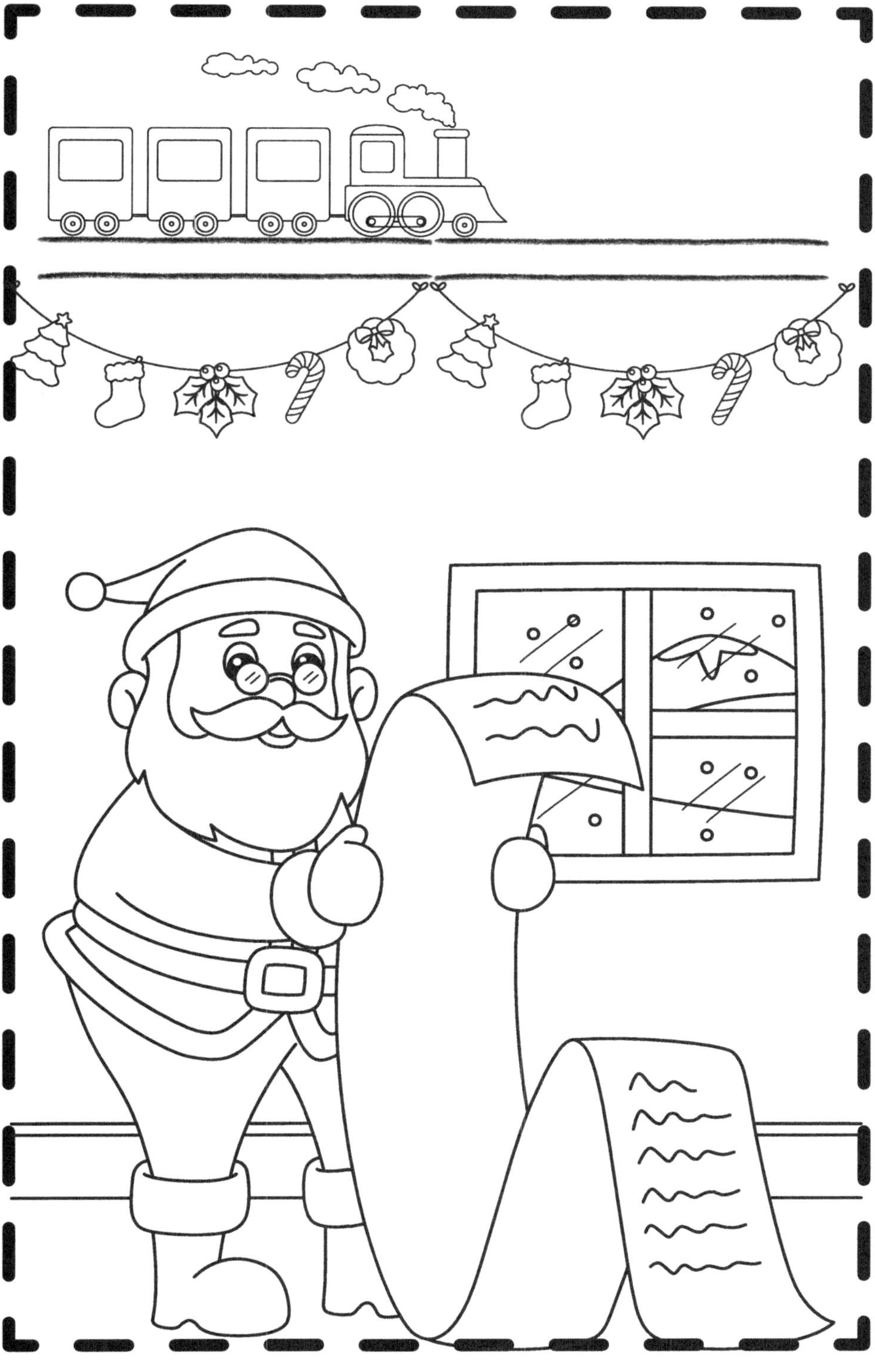

R I have rings and needles. What am I?

J What do you call a candy that sings?

J What is it called on Christmas Day after all the presents have been opened?

A Christmas tree. / A wrapper. / A Christmess.

Sweater Weather

J Why did the egg nog go to school?

J
A: Knock Knock.
B: Who's there?
A: Alpaca.
B: Alpaca who?
A: Alpaca the winter coats, it's getting cold outside.

T Name the reindeer whose names begin with D.

It wanted to get egg-ucated. / Dasher, Dancer, Donner.

Warm and Cozy

J What do the elves call Santa when he's on break?

R Red and white, I curve just right. A festive treat, both day and night. What am I?

T What is Frosty the Snowman's nose made out of?

Santa Pause / A candy cane / A button

For Christmas I ate...

What year does New Year's Day come before Christmas?

Where does a snowman keep his money?

I'm sweet and twisted, and red and white. What am I?

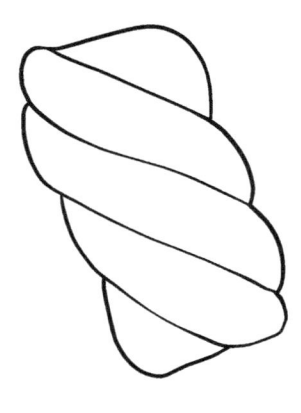

Every year! / in a snowbank / A candy cane

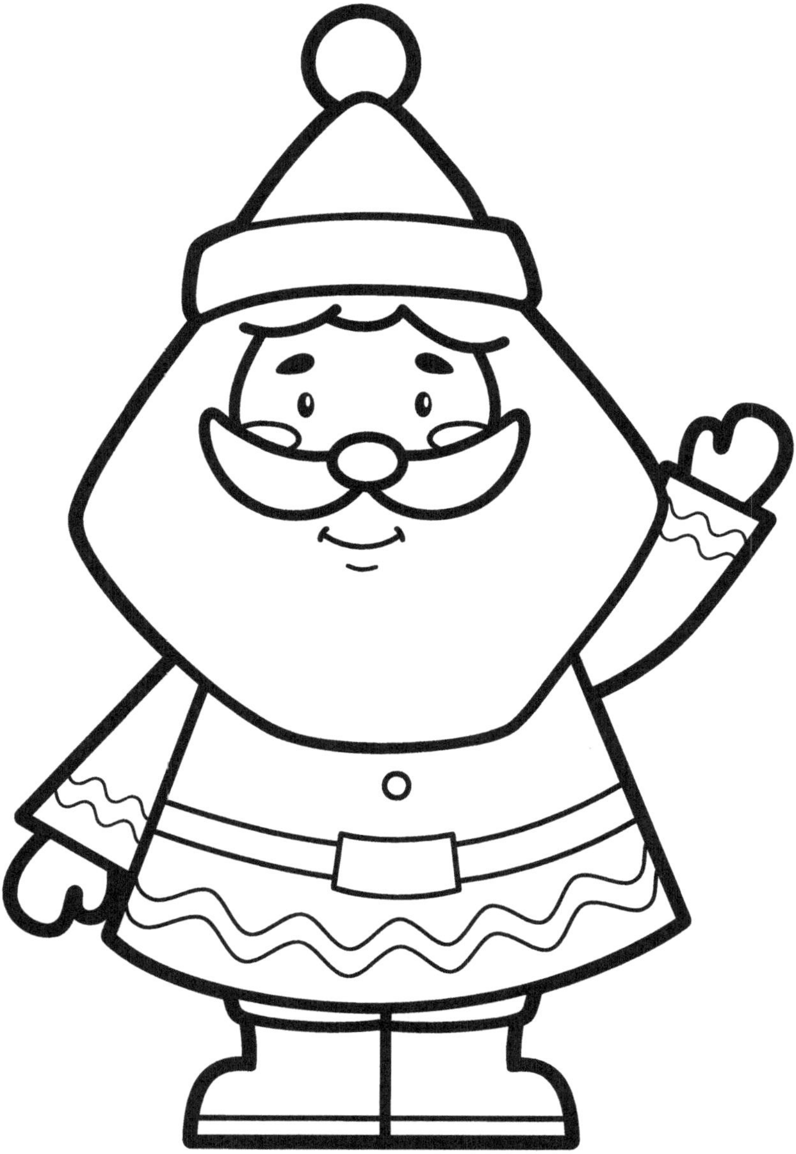

J Why did Mrs. Clause put wheels on her rocking chair?

T Which country started the tradition of putting up a Christmas tree?

J What do snowmen eat for breakfast?

She wanted to rock and roll! / Germany / Ice Krispies

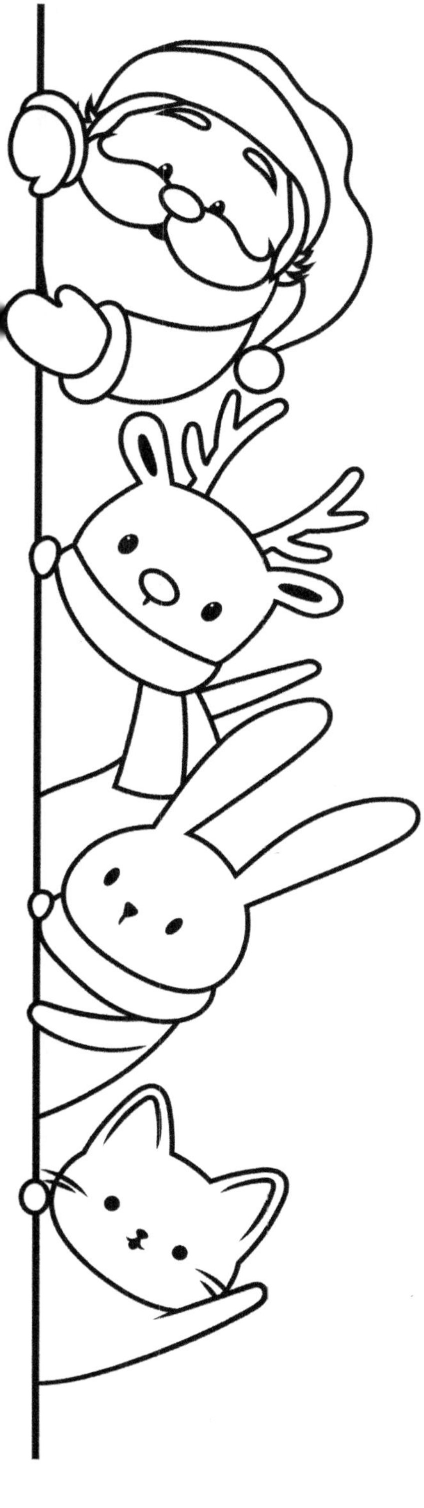

J: Why don't they play hide and seek at the North Pole?

WP: 6 kids made 6 snowmen. If each kid made an equal number of snowmen, how many snowmen did each kid make?

Because good luck hiding when there's nowhere to hide! / 1

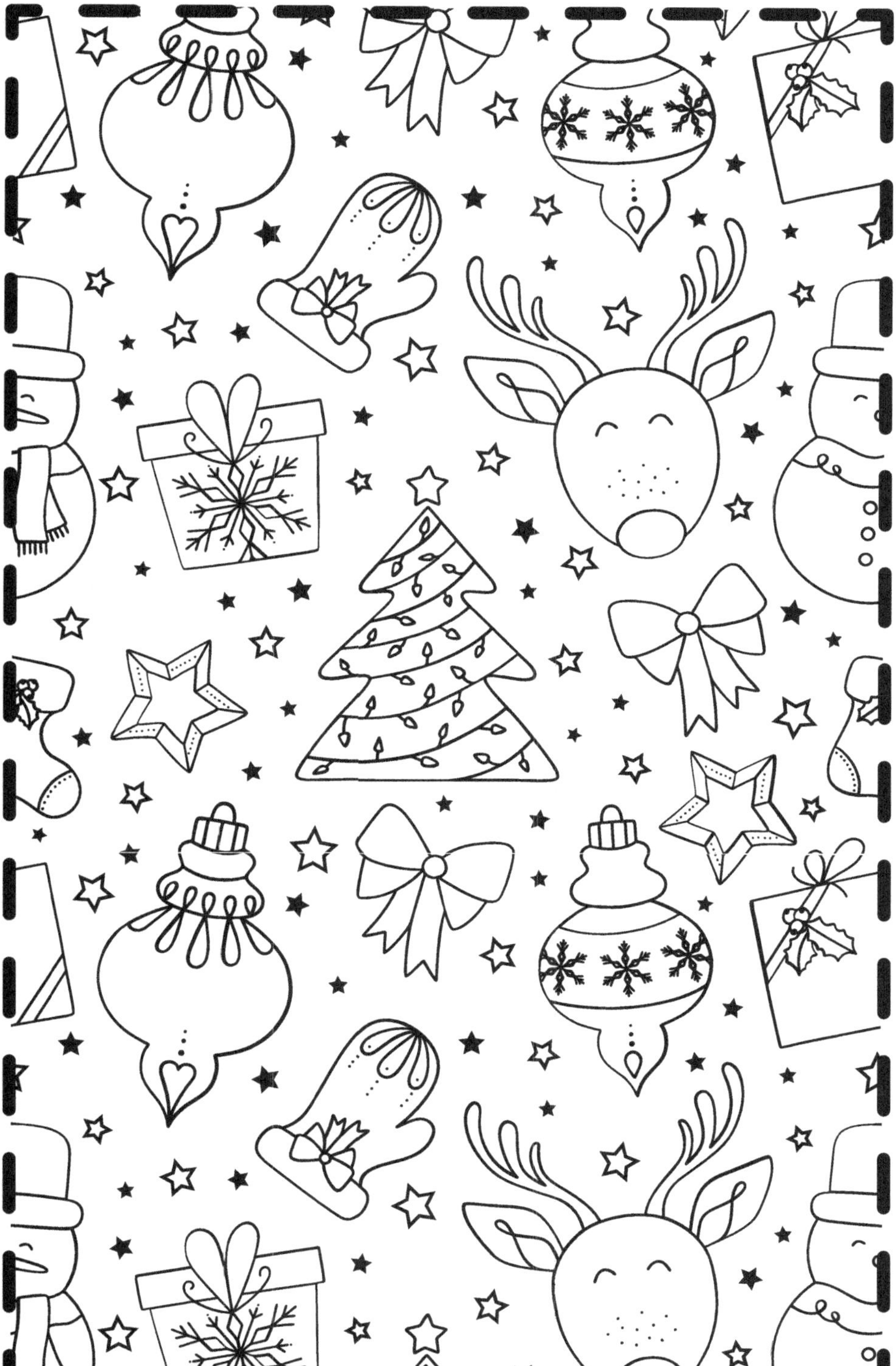

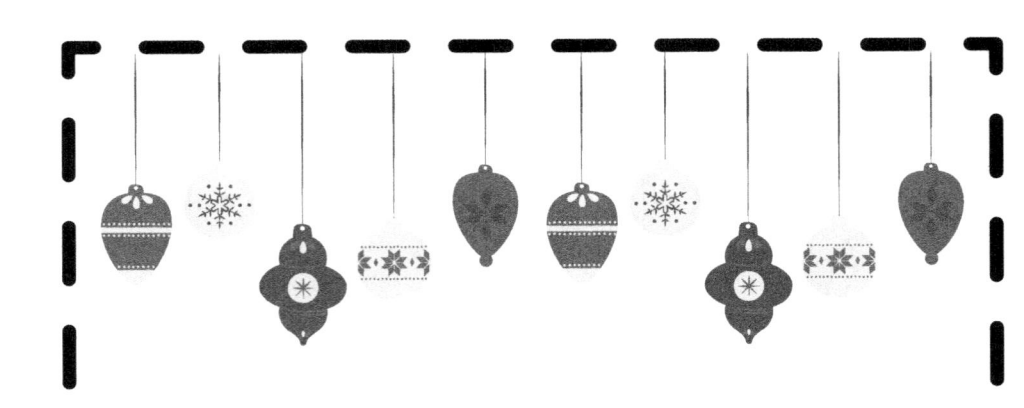

J What did one ornament say to another?

T How many reindeer does Santa have?

R Green and round, on the door I am found. What am I?

"I like hanging with you." / 9 / A wreath

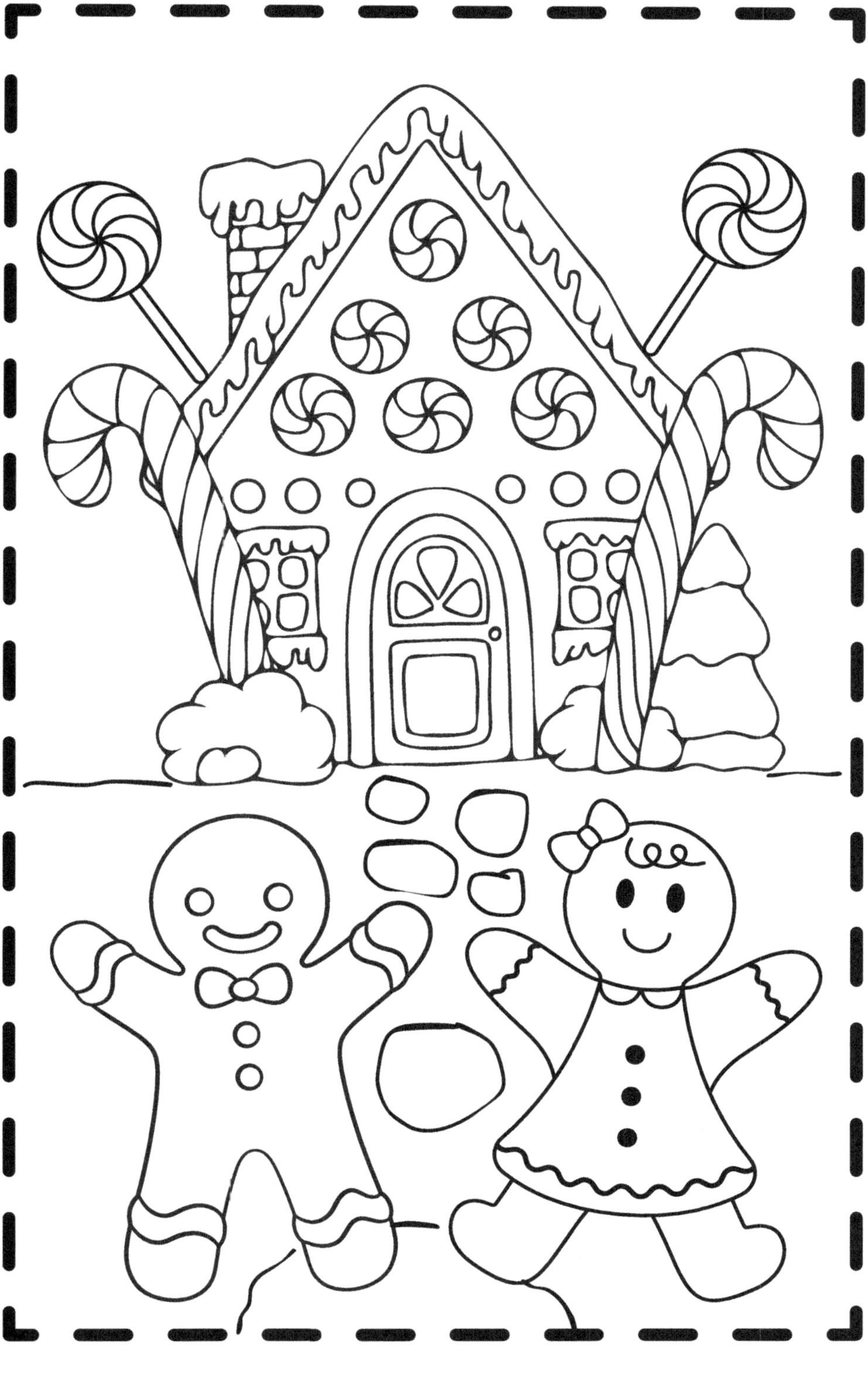

R What comes at the end of Christmas Day?

J What is your parent's favorite Christmas Carol?

WP Santa has one sack with a pound of Christmas cards and another sack with a pound of toys. Which sack weighs more?

The letter "Y" / Silent Night / They both weigh 1 pound

Merry & Bright

WP There are 8 gifts in a sack. Eight people each take 1 gift, but there is still 1 gift in the sack. How can this be?

R What has a head, a tail, but no body?

The 8th person took the sack with one gift still in it. / A Christmas coin.

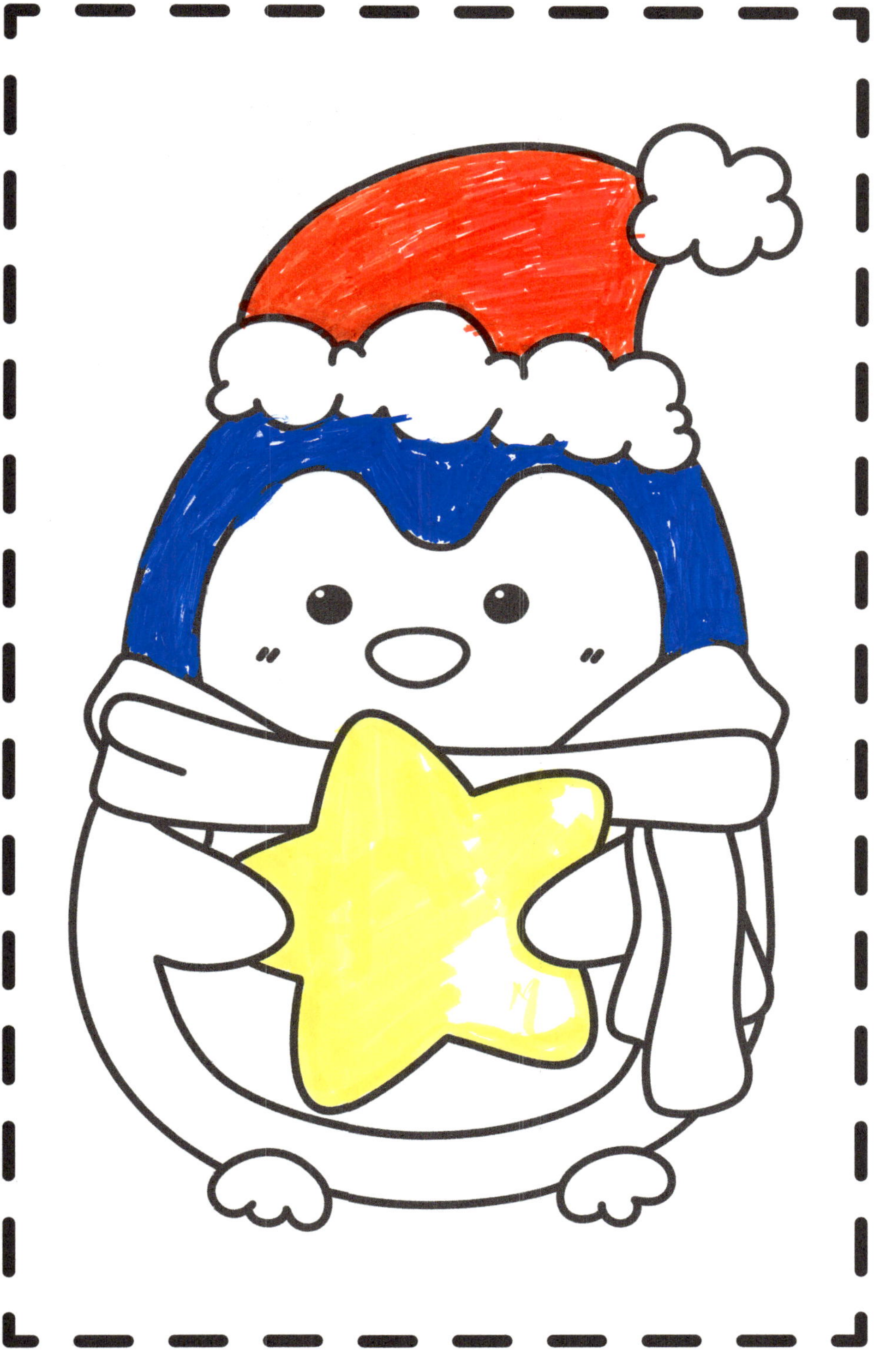

R What falls, but never gets hurt?

J Why did the gift go to school?

R Hung by the fire, filled with delights, Gifts peek out, in the silent night. What am I?

Snow. / It had to give a present-ation! / A stocking

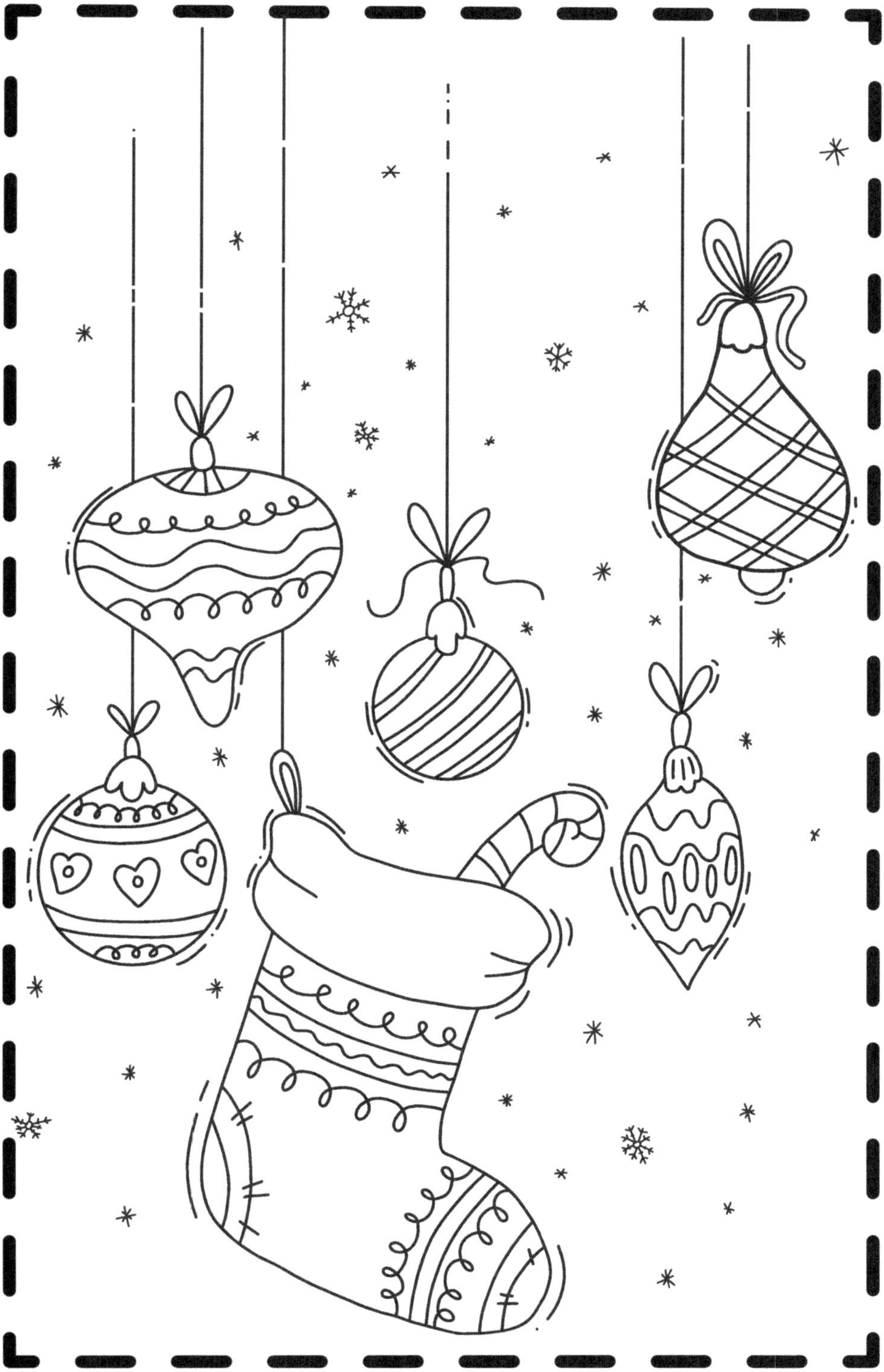

J What do you call a very old snowman?

J What did the elf say to the mummy on Christmas?

T In Sweden, what animal does Santa Clause ride?

A puddle. / You better wrap it up. / A goat.

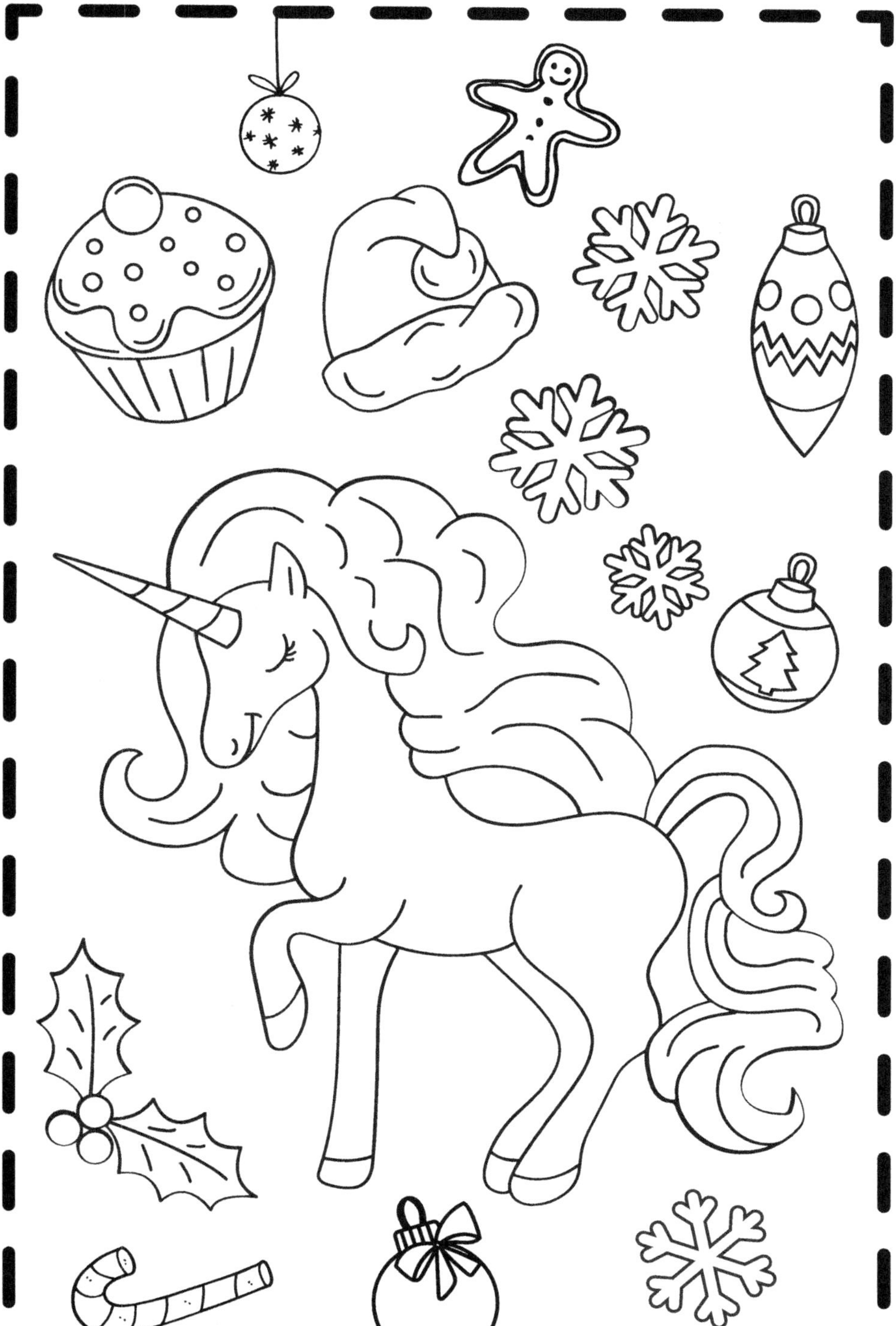

What's an elf's favorite sport?

What do you get when Santa goes down a chimney while a fire is lit?

North Ploe-vaulting! / Crisp Kringle

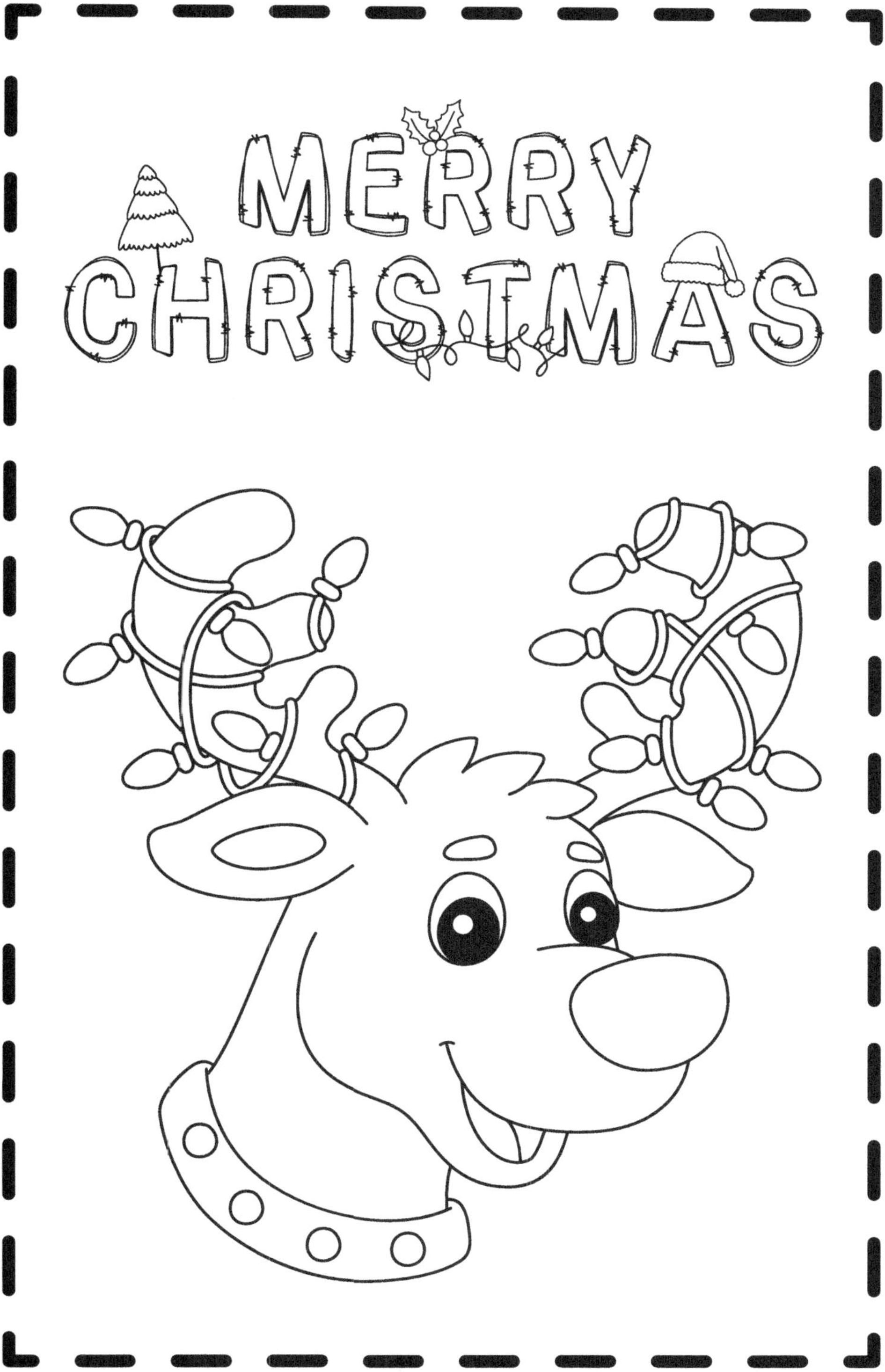
MERRY
CHRISTMAS

T
What's the name of a Christmas cake that symbolizes a log burnt on Christmas Eve?

WP
You've ordered pizza for Christmas dinner for eight. How many times do you need to cut the pizza to get eight slices?

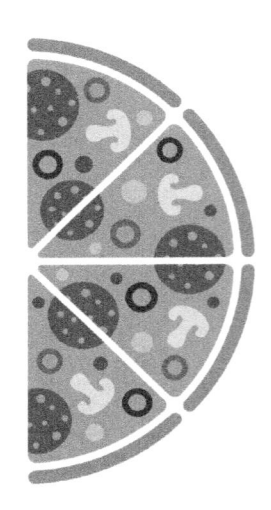

J
What did Santa call the greedy elf that stole all the presents?

A Yule log. / 4 / So Elfish!

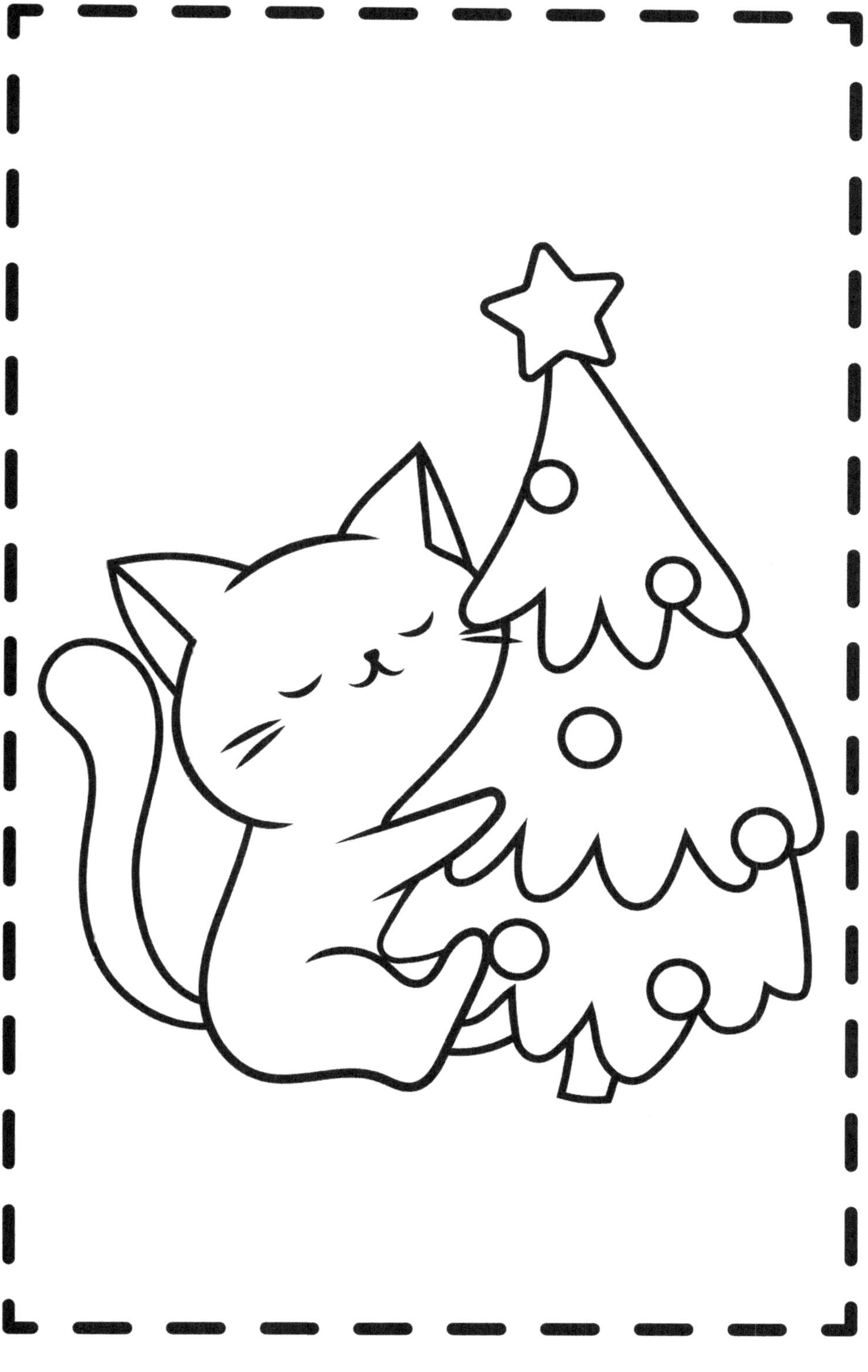

A: Knock knock.
B: Who's there?
A: Mary.
B: Mary who?
A: Mary Christmas to you!

What was Santa's best subject at school?

Chemis-tree

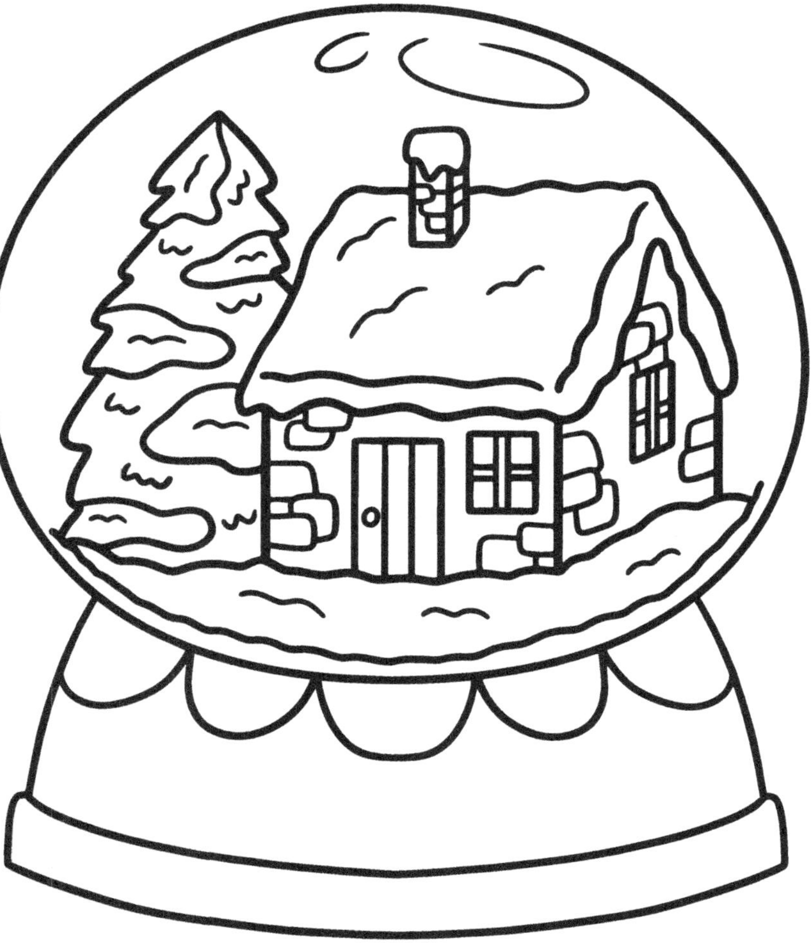

J Why is Christmas so cold?

T What is the shape of a candy cane represent?

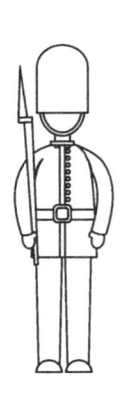

J What do you get when you cross a guard with a duck?

It's Decemberrr. / A shepherd's staff / A nut quacker!

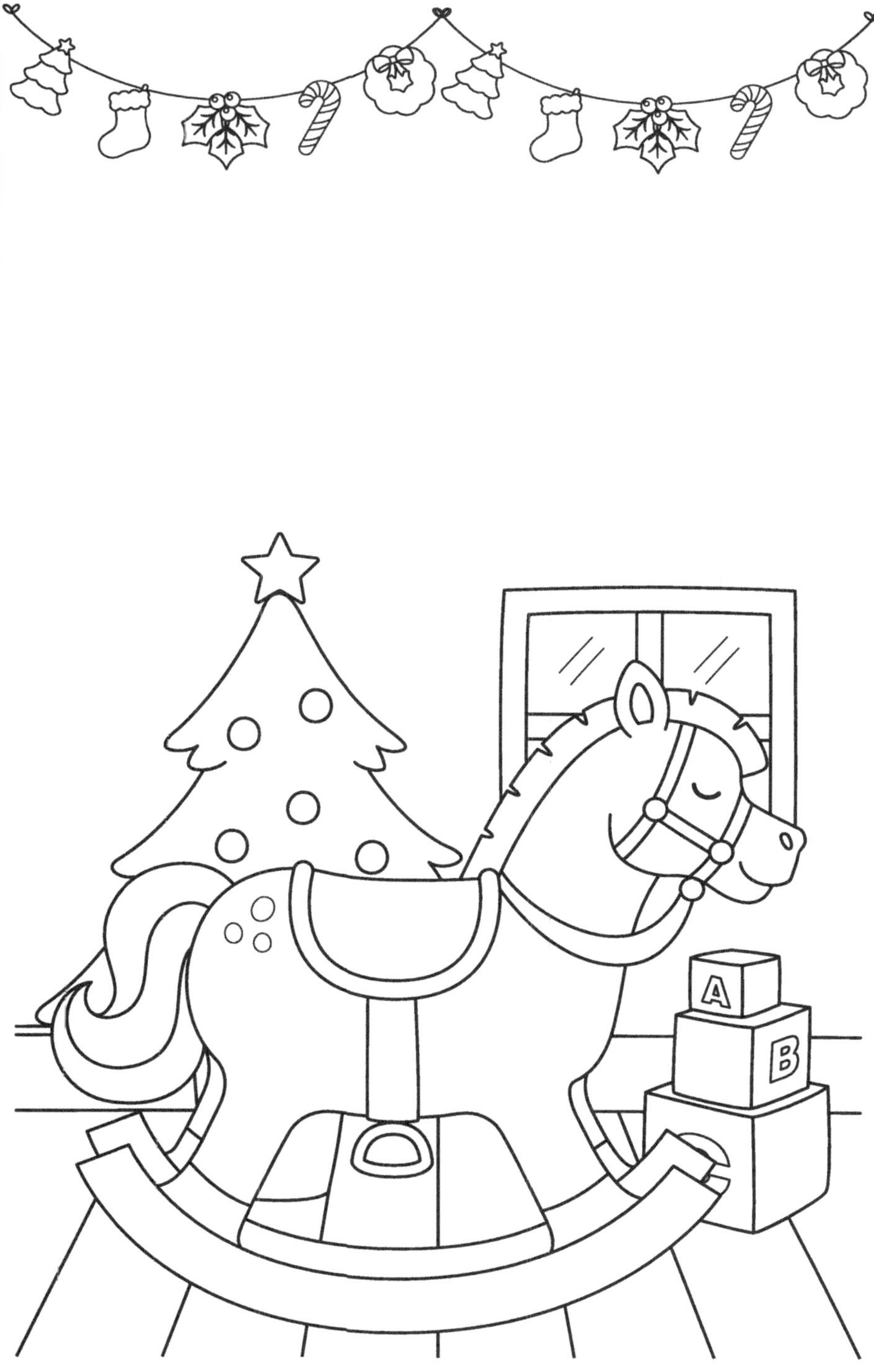
A
B

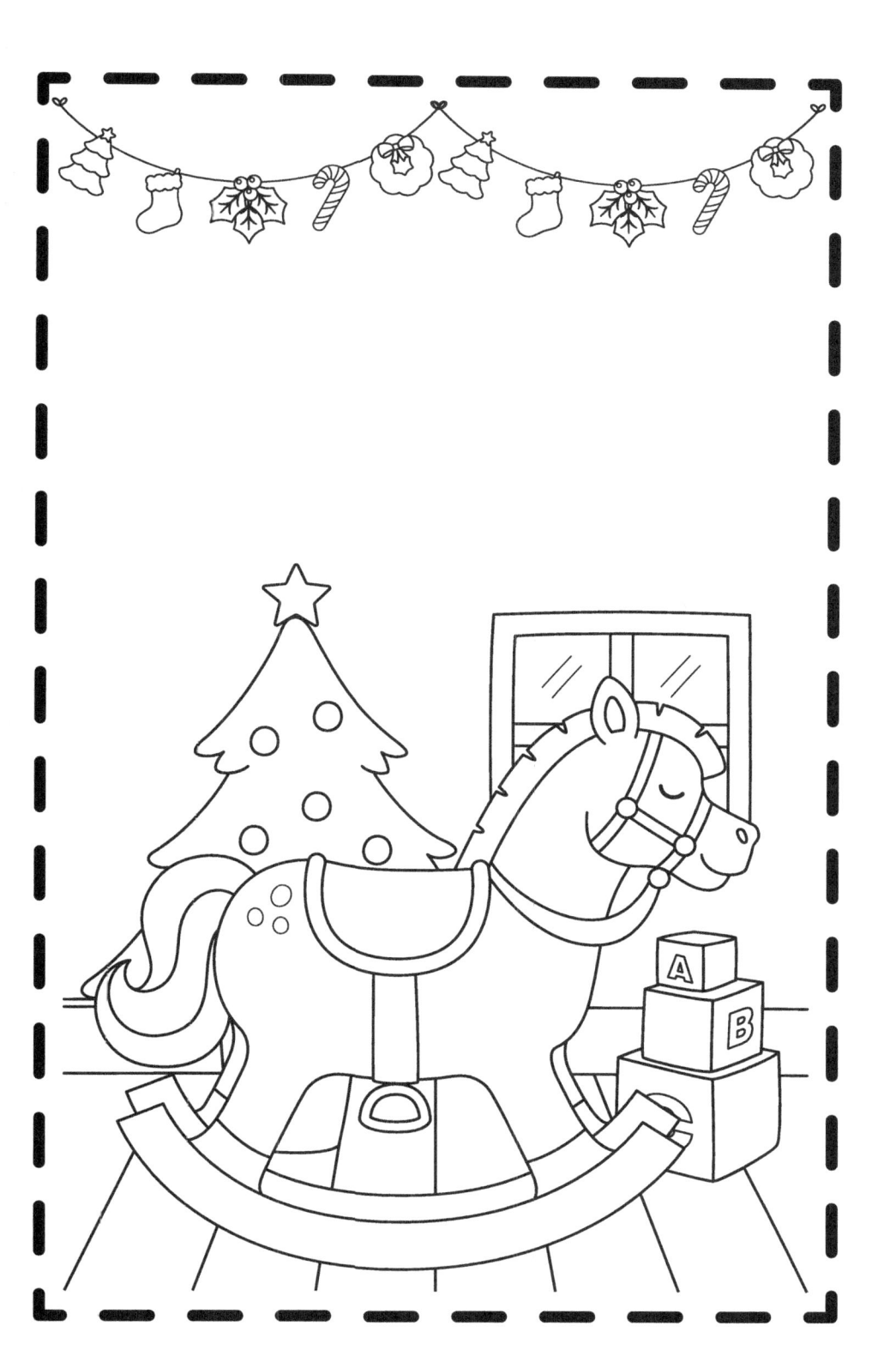

What do cows say to each other at midnight on New Year's?

Why didn't Rudolph want to show his parents his report card?

Two moms and two daughters went out for Christmas brunch and each ate one portion. Only three portions were eaten in total, how is this possible?

Happy Moo-year! / Becasue he went down in history. / A Grandmother (who is a mother), mother (who is a mother and a daughter), and daughter.

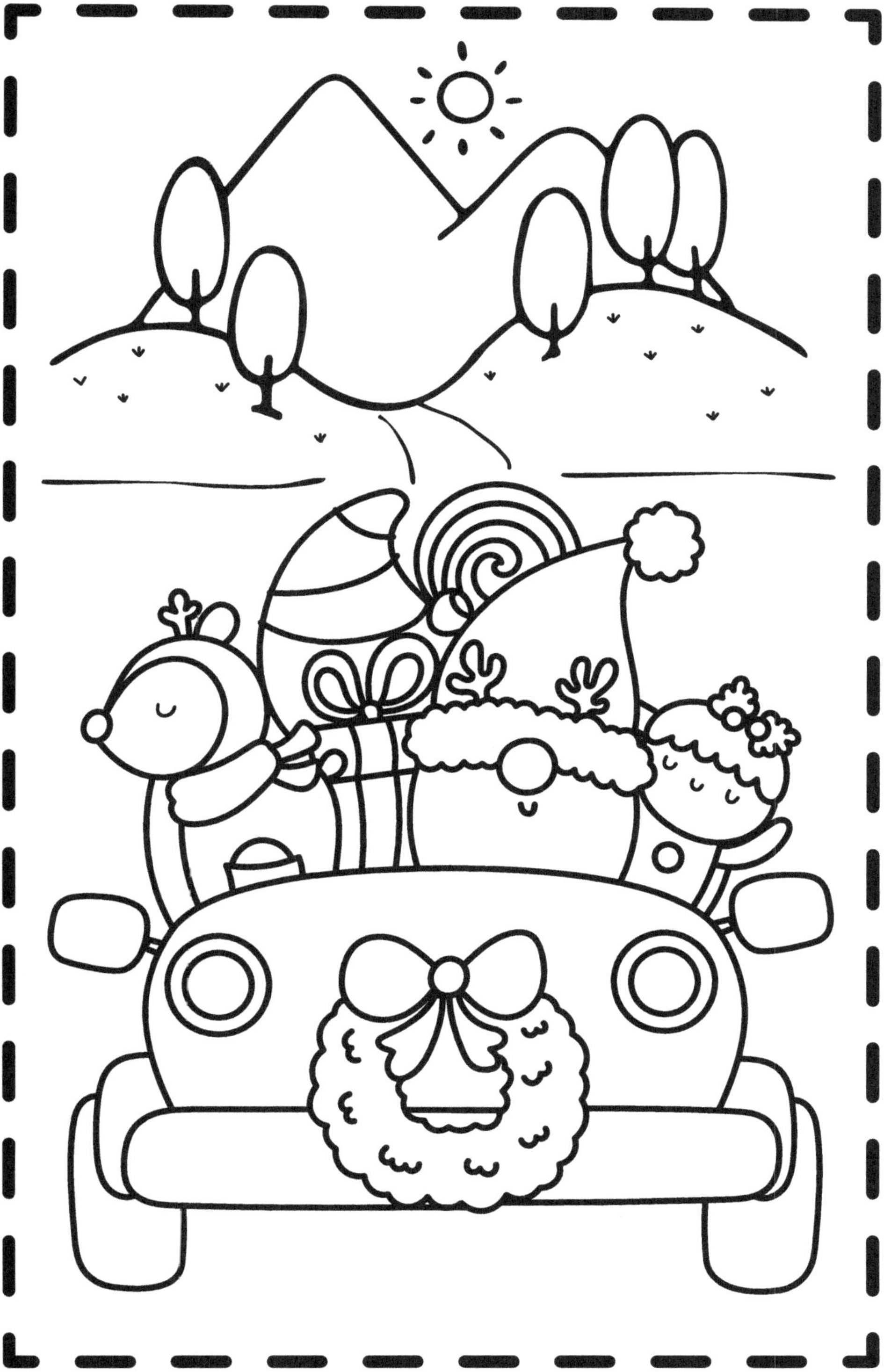

What did one Christmas angel say to the other?

Why would a snowman look inside a bag of carrots?

Who wrote the book *How the Grinch Stole Christmas*?

Halo there! / He was picking his nose! / Dr. Seuss

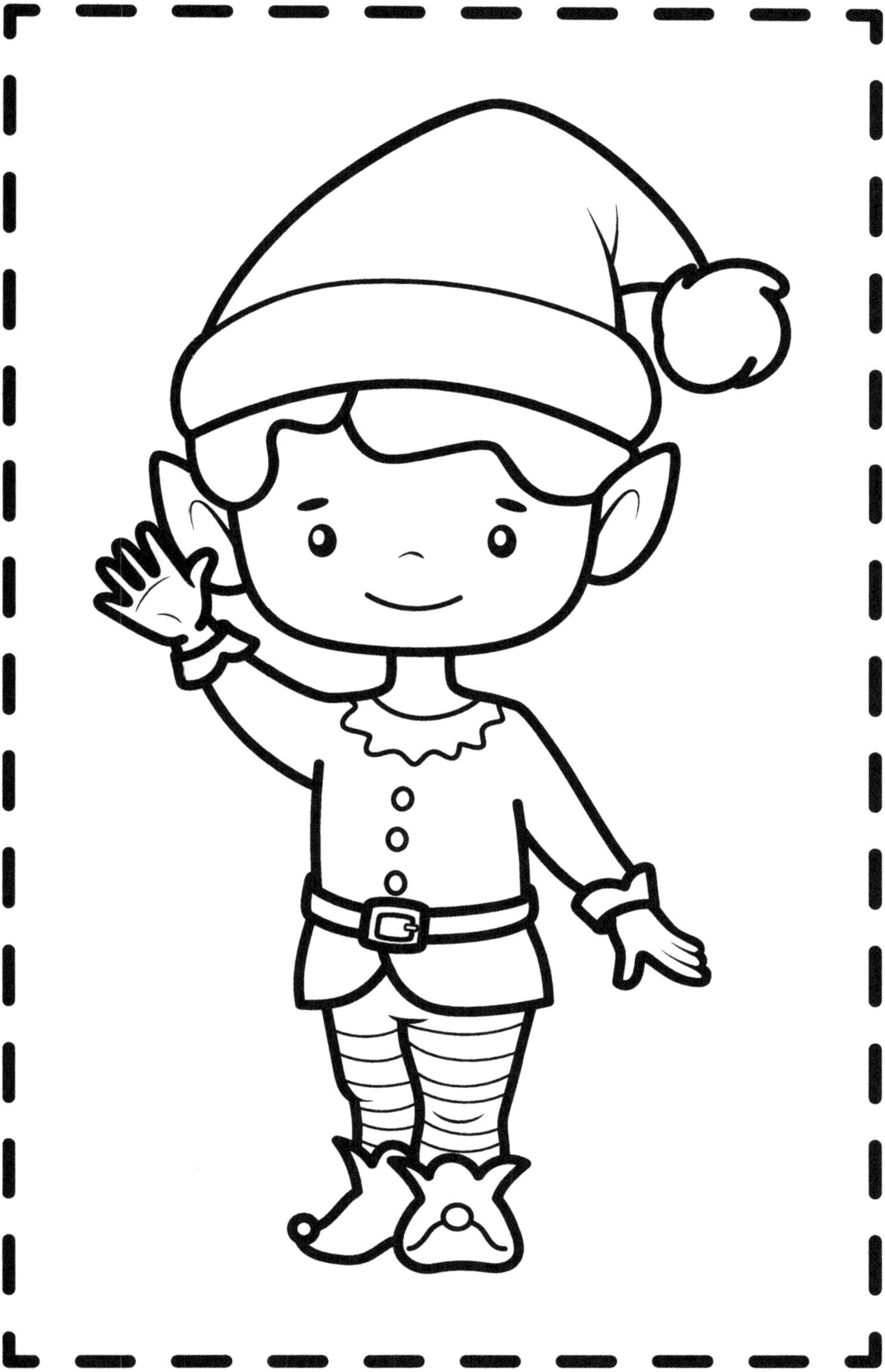

T What are the silver strands used to decorate a Christmas tree called?

J What happened to the thief that stole Christmas?

J Why are Christmas trees so bad at knitting?

Tinsel. / He got 12 months. / Because they always lose their needles!

My Christmas wish:

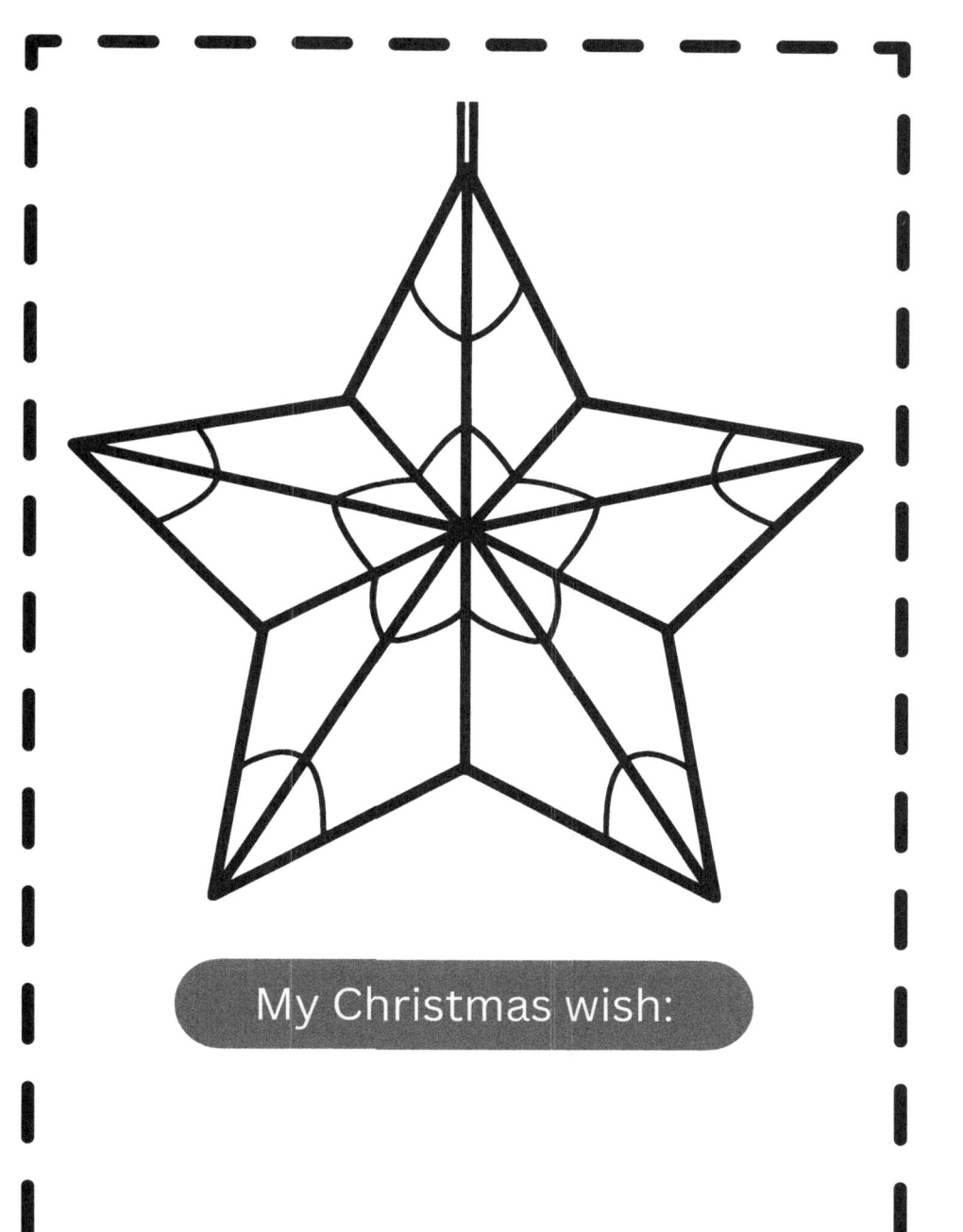

T What do *Harry Potter*, *The Lord of the Rings* and Christmas all have in common?

R On Christmas, I can be easily caught, but never thrown.

T Which classic fairytale inspired the gingerbread house?

They all have elves! / A cold. / Hansel and Gretel

Happy New Year
Happy
Happy New Year
New Year
Happy
Happy New Year
Happy
Happy New Year

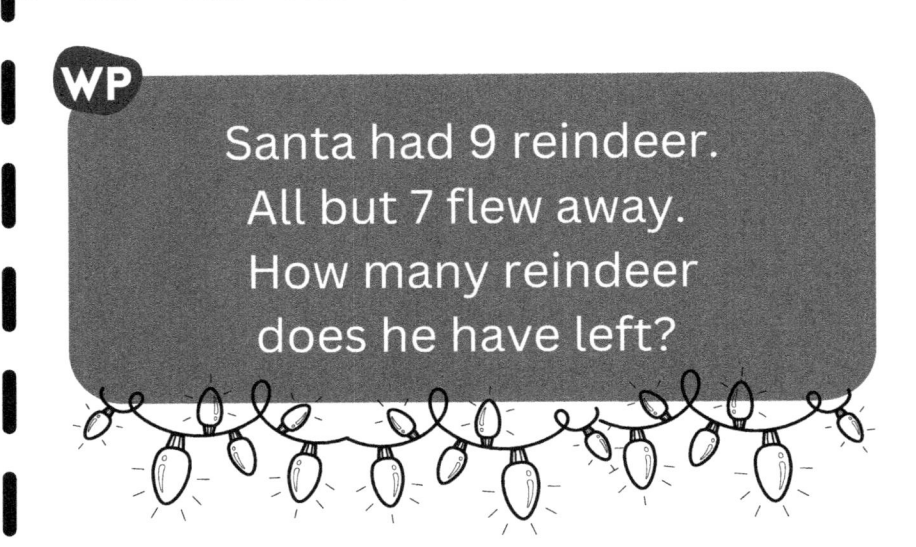

WP Santa had 9 reindeer. All but 7 flew away. How many reindeer does he have left?

What did the beaver say to the Christmas tree? **J**

Who has eyes made of coal? **T**

7. / Nice gnawing you! / Frosty the Snowman

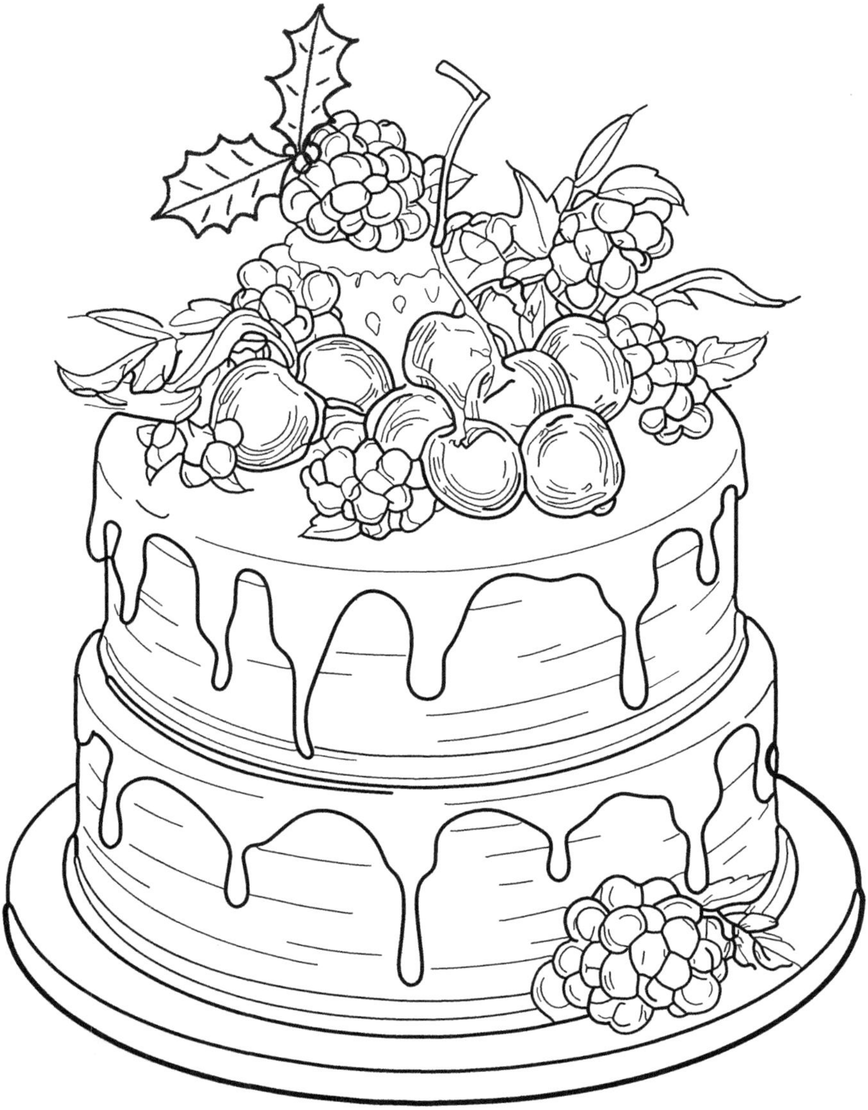

WP There are four presents, and you take 3. How many do you have?

J What does Santa use to keep his breath fresh?

R Inside a sphere, winter scenes unfold. Shake me up, and watch the magic I behold. What am I?

3. / Orna-mints / A snow globe.

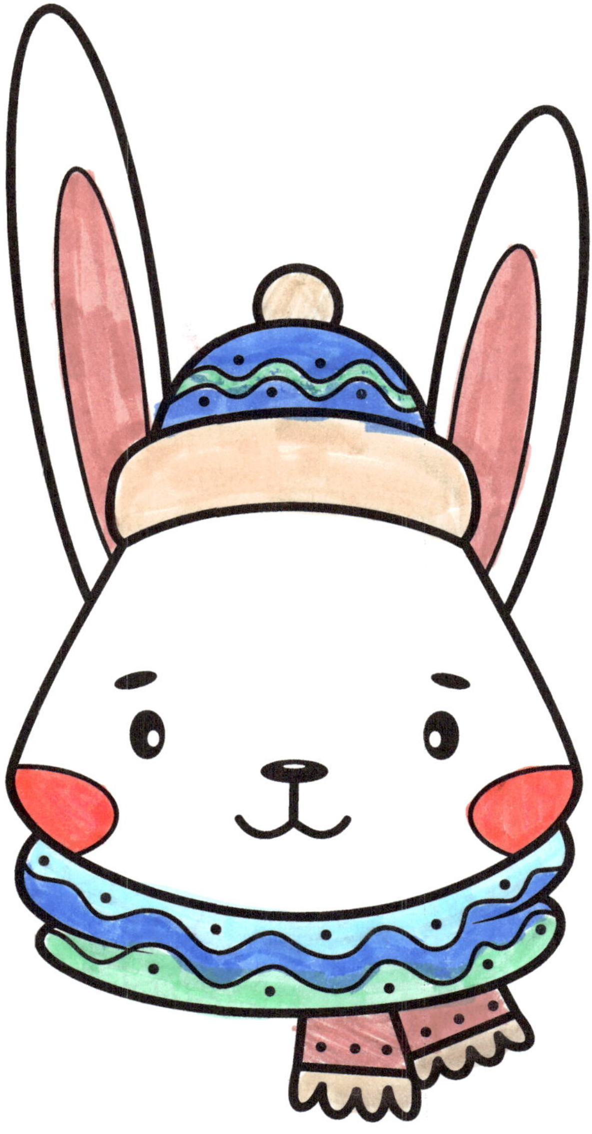

J
A: Knock knock.
B: Who's there?
A: Holly.
B: Holly who?
A: Holly-days are here again! Time to be merry!

J
Where do girl reindeer go to find a boyfriend?

T
Which one of Santa's reindeer shares the name of a Valentine's Day icon?

Star-bucks. / Cupid

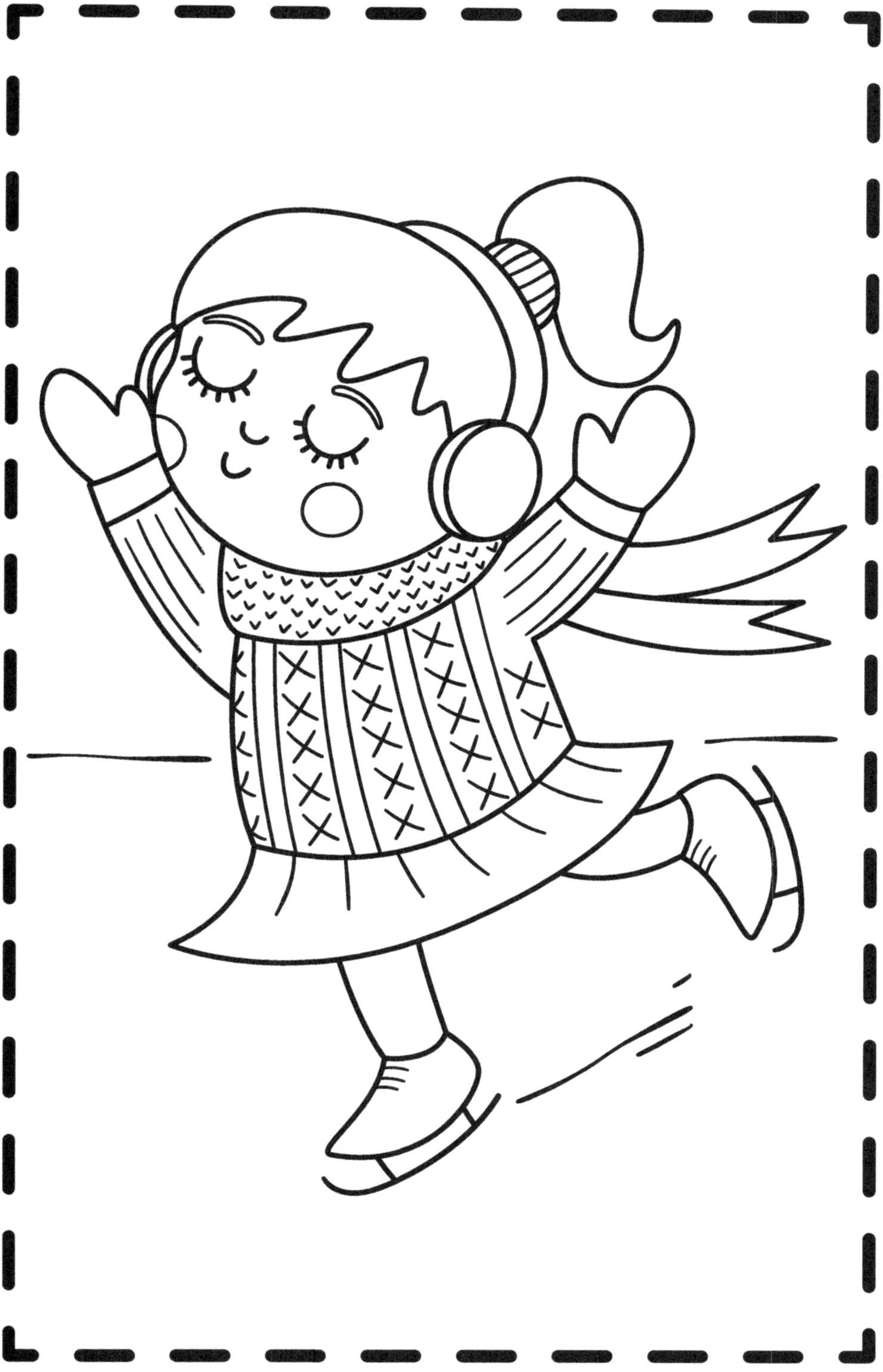

J What did one snowman say to the other snowman?

T What is Santa's favorties snack?

Mom is a Christmas tree. Dad is an apple tree. What kind of tree is their baby? **R**

Smells like carrots! / Cookies / A pineapple tree!

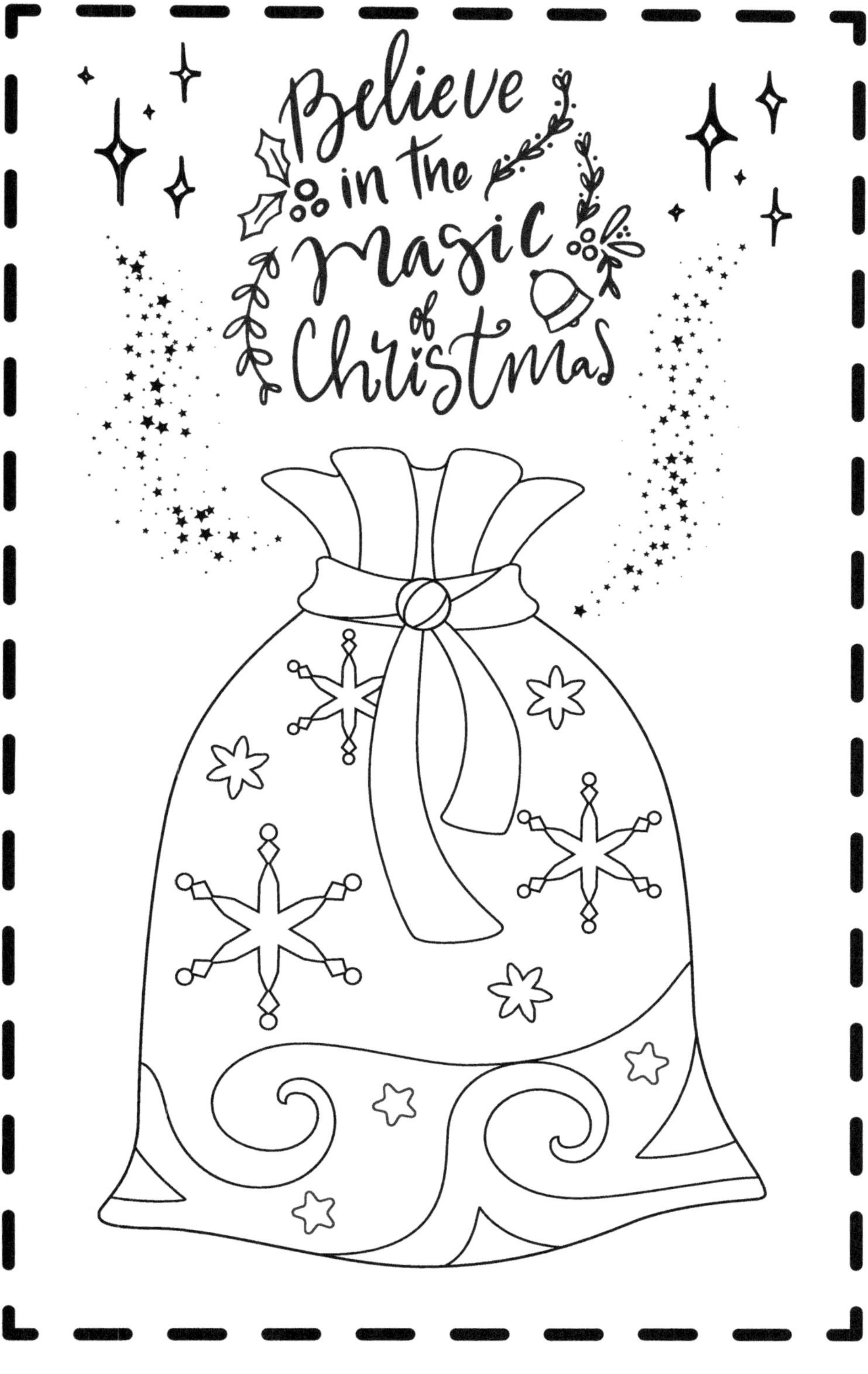
Believe in the magic of Christmas

Printed in Great Britain
by Amazon